FIFE COUNCIL LIBRARIES

FB014871

KT-584-390

WORLD ISSUES

CHINA
The New Superpower?

  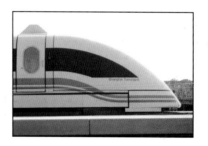

A look at the way the world is today

Antony Mason

Re
by
in

Franklin Watts
London • Sydney

ABOUT THIS BOOK

CHINA is developing fast into one of the world's greatest industrial nations. It is a remarkable achievement for a country that was barely able to feed itself 30 years ago. New wealth promises much to China's vast population and the effects can be felt right across the globe. But can China's economic boom be sustained, and is the Communist government capable of steering the country into the future? This book explores how these huge changes came about, and whether China really can become the next superpower.

New edition printed in 2006
© Aladdin Books Ltd 2005
Produced by Aladdin Books Ltd
2/3 Fitzroy Mews, London W1T 6DF

ISBN 978–07496–6266–0 (Hardback)
ISBN 978–07496–7014–6 (Paperback)

First published in 2005 by

Franklin Watts	Franklin Watts Australia
338 Euston Road	Hachette Children's Books
London	Level 17/207 Kent Street
NW1 3BH	Sydney NSW 2000

Designers: Pete Bennett – PBD; Flick, Book Design and Graphics
Editor: Katie Harker
Picture research: Harker & Bennett
Editorial consultant: Professor Peter Preston, Department of Political Science and International Studies, University of Birmingham, UK.

The author, Antony Mason, is a freelance editor and author of more than sixty books for both children and adults.

All rights reserved   Printed in Malaysia

A CIP catalogue record for this book is available from the British Library.

Dewey Classification: 951.06

CONTENTS

INTRODUCTION

Look around you. There is probably something made in China close at hand: a pencil, an item of clothing, a calculator. Over the last 25 years, China has turned into one of the world's greatest manufacturers. Recently, its economy has grown at a phenomenal rate of 10 per cent a year – five times the rate of most Western countries. In the 1970s, China was an impoverished Third-World country. Now it ranks amongst the six largest world economies – and many international companies have dashed to get their foot in the door of China's booming market.

Commuters cycle into China's capital city, Beijing. The city now boasts over seven million residents.

THE GIANT AWAKENS

Perhaps this should be no surprise, given the statistics. With 1.3 billion people, China has the largest population in the world – one in every five human beings is Chinese – a population more than four times that of the USA. China is also the third largest country (after Russia and Canada) in terms of land area.

The Chinese civilisation – once one of the most advanced and sophisticated on Earth – stretches back at least four thousand years. But the last two centuries have been deeply troubled. The policies of the Communist government (from 1949) created a destitute population who were scared of the police state. To the outside world, China was mysterious and unpredictable. China also had a huge army with nuclear weapons.

But in the late 1970s, the Chinese government changed its policies. With its huge and inexpensive workforce, China suddenly began to make products at a fraction of the price charged by other countries. By attracting the world's traders, China also attracted international industries, with their new ideas and technologies.

RAPID CHANGE

Since then, the cities of China have grown at a colossal speed – harbouring a new generation of young Chinese who are well-educated and ambitious. China now has many millionaires – an idea that would have been unthinkable 25 years ago.

But this rapid change has come at a cost as the gap between rich and poor has widened. The poor are swarming to the cities in the hope of finding work – often to be disappointed by their living and working conditions. At the same time, farmers in the country fear that they have become trapped in poverty.

Meanwhile, China wants to demonstrate its status as a leading player on the world stage. Following the collapse of the Soviet Union in 1991, the USA became the only real superpower – with influence over political and military events in the world. Future changes in economic strength, military power and alliances will continue to affect the balances of power between nations. The question is: has China got what it takes to become the next superpower?

The 2008 Olympic Games

In the closing ceremony of the Olympic Games in Athens in 2004, China invited the world's athletes to the 2008 Olympic Games in Beijing. To back up this invitation, Chinese performers mounted a spectacular display designed to represent the new China: confident, stylish and an eager participant in the modern world. The Chinese will spend more on the Games (£60 billion) than any previous host in order to demonstrate to the world – and billions of television viewers – what China can do, in building, organisation and sport.

Work is already well advanced on the Olympic facilities in Beijing, including ultra-modern stadiums designed by top international architects, in concert with Chinese designers and construction companies. For instance, the main stadium, nicknamed the 'Bird's Nest', has been designed by Herzog and De Meuron, the Swiss partnership that was also responsible for the Tate Modern building in London.

China not only wants to host a brilliant Games, it also wants to come out top in the medal league. It stands a fair chance of success having come second in Athens in 2004. Its 3,000 special sports schools have already started to train champions of the future.

Shanghai – China's largest city and financial capital – is bristling with ultra-modern buildings, designed by some of the world's top architects. However, many residents are still living in poverty.

KAZAKHSTAN

KYRGYZSTAN

TAJIKISTAN

RUSSIAN
FEDERATION

MONGOLIA

CHINA

N.KOREA

S.KOREA

JAPAN

PAKISTAN

BHUTAN

MYANMAR
(BURMA)

HONG KONG

NEPAL

LAOS

TAIWAN

INDIA

VIETNAM

PHILIPPINES

BANGLADESH

THAILAND

CAMBODIA

MALAYSIA

INDONESIA

MAP OF CHINA

China's cities and provinces

China has 32 cities with a population of over a million. Most of these cities are in the east of the country. About 400 million Chinese live in cities while 900 million live in the rural areas. The ten largest cities are outlined below (population figures are for cities themselves, and do not include the surrounding urban areas).

Shanghai 9 million
Beijing (Peking) 7.1 million
Tianjin (Tientsin) 4.3 million
Wuhan (Hankow) 4 million
Shenyang 3.5 million
Guangzhou (Canton) 3.4 million
Nanjing 2.8 million

Harbin 2.7 million
Xian 2.6 million
Chongqing (Chungking) 2.3 million

China is divided into 22 provinces (or 23 if Taiwan is included) plus 5 autonomous regions (e.g. Tibet, Inner Mongolia, shown in bold) and 4 municipalities (e.g. Beijing, Shanghai, shown underlined).

Full name: The People's Republic of China (PRC)
Capital: Beijing
Population: 1.3 billion
Land area: 9,561,000 square kilometres
Language: Mandarin (92 per cent of the population), Cantonese, Wu, Hakka and hundreds of dialects (but the written language is the same for all).
Currency: Renminbi ('People's Currency'), in which 1 yuan is divided into 100 fen.

8

The Chinese language

Chinese written words look very different to those of other languages. They were based originally on 'pictograms' (or pictographs) – simple, standardized drawings that represented essential words, such as 'man', 'horse' or 'water'. Over time, additions to the basic pictograms produced many more new words and meanings. Chinese dictionaries may contain more than 40,000 of these 'characters'.

The average educated Chinese person knows between five and ten thousand characters but the learning process is extremely long. Given the difficulty of learning characters, and the negative impact this has on the general level of literacy, the Chinese government announced, in 1954, that a couple of thousand of the most common characters were to be simplified. Many parts of China (and also Singapore) use simplified Chinese, but Hong Kong and Taiwan, as well as the majority of overseas Chinese, continue to use the older, traditional forms.

The geography of China

China has a long coast – stretching 6,400 kilometres – on the Pacific Ocean, running from its icy northern border with North Korea to the tropical warmth of the South China Sea. To the west, China stretches 3,000 kilometres into the heart of Asia, across vast agricultural lands, desert, plains and mountains, rising to the Himalayas in the southwest. In the north, straddling the border with Mongolia, is the vast Gobi desert, hot in summer and bitterly cold in winter. The most northerly part of China is Manchuria, in the northeast, rimmed by the border with Russia.

Three great rivers run across China from the inland regions: the Huang He (Yellow River) in the north; the Chang Jiang (Yangtze) in central China; and, in the south, the Xi Jiang, which forms the Zhu Jiang (Pearl River) near its delta on the coast.

The climate of China is essentially dry in winter and wet in summer. Temperatures range from well below freezing to swelteringly hot, depending on the season, latitude and height above sea level. Wheat is generally grown in the north, and rice – which needs a warmer climate – in the south.

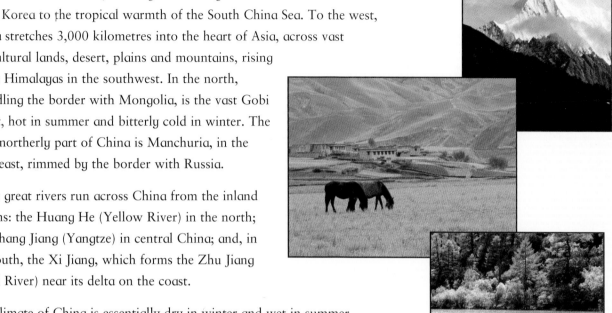

9

AN ANCIENT CIVILISATION

China boasts one of the oldest continuous civilisations in the world – and once, one of the most advanced. The Chinese were the first to make silk, cast iron, paper, fireworks, porcelain and navigational compasses, amongst other things. When the Italian explorer Marco Polo visited China, in 1275-92, he was amazed at what he saw. The history of China is one of unity and division. China's vast size and varied population has always made it difficult to hold together as a single nation. Dynasties of powerful emperors managed to unify China for a while – but then the empire would break up into warring factions. Keeping the whole nation under central control remains a key issue to this day.

IMPERIAL CHINA

Qin Shi Huangdi is generally considered to be the first emperor (reigned 221-210 BC) founding the Qin dynasty. Qin (or Ch'in) is the origin of the word 'China'. When he died, Qin Shi Huangdi was buried in a massive tomb complex in his capital city of Xian, surrounded by lifesize pottery soldiers, the so-called 'Terracotta Army'. Six major dynasties followed the Qin dynasty – the Han, Tang, Song, Yuan, Ming and Qing dynasties. The Chinese emperors were in constant fear of invasion. They built the Great Wall of China – a 6,400 km defence barrier – to keep enemies out. One massive invasion occurred in 1207, when Genghis Khan and his army of Mongolian horsemen stormed across the Great Wall and captured northern China, before creating a vast empire stretching to the borders of Europe, and founding the Yuan dynasty.

Confucianism

Life in Imperial China was strongly influenced by a philosophy called Confucianism. Based on the teachings of Kongfuzi (c.551-479 BC) – known as Confucius in the West – Confucianism sets out a way of life based on morality, obedience, and respect for one's parents, ancestors and the State. It was believed that this would provide stability and order for the good of all society. One of the great strengths of Chinese imperial rule was the fact that almost anyone could become a member of the administration – education was rewarded and civil servants were appointed on the basis of merit.

The Great Wall of China took centuries to build. It was started in 221 BC and reached its final length during the Ming dynasty (1368-1644).

The Chinese emperors considered that they were ordained by the gods to rule. Their unique culture – quite distinctive from those of their neighbours – was the cornerstone of Chinese identity, and of their sense of superiority. The Chinese also believed that they were the only civilised people on Earth, and foreigners were effectively barbarians. This explains why the Chinese have not generally been aggressive empire-builders. When expanding their empire, emperors tended to concentrate more on shoring up the borders with their less civilised neighbours; they did not try to create colonies on distant continents.

That said, the Chinese have had very distant trading links since ancient times, especially by sea to other parts of Asia. The overland trading route that spanned the middle of Asia, known as the Silk Roads, connected China to Ancient Greece and Rome, and continued to operate throughout history.

Admiral Zheng He

In 1405, a Chinese admiral called Zheng He (Cheng Ho) began a series of exploratory sailing expeditions. Zheng He reached India and Africa, but after his death in 1435, China turned its back on world exploration.

The 1400s saw the start of the Great Age of European Exploration. The Spanish funded Christopher Columbus, who sailed to the Americas in 1492, and Vasco da Gama, from Portugal, found the sea route round Africa to India in 1497-99. History might well have been different if China had continued to explore and joined in the rush to spread world trade and imperial power.

Many of the historic buildings found in China today bear the architectural style of China's imperial rulers.

11

The Terracotta Army – part of the tomb complex of emperor Qin Shi Huangdi – is one of the world's great archaeological treasures.

The Opium Wars

To the Chinese Imperial government, opium was an illegal evil that was turning its citizens into drug addicts. To the British, opium was a useful trade commodity – produced cheaply in India and sold in China. In 1839, Chinese officials seized 20,000 cases of British opium in Guangzhou. The British were outraged and attacked Guangzhou, quickly defeating the Chinese who were forced to sign a trade agreement. A similar squabble in the 1850s led to China giving Western traders access to inland China. These wars caused deep resentment in China, and a lasting suspicion of outsiders.

THE BARBARIANS ARRIVE

The last of the great Chinese dynasties, the Qing (or Manchu) dynasty (1644-1911) coincided with Europe's rapid expansion of trade and aggressive empire-building. The British, French, Portuguese, Spanish and Dutch were busy claiming colonies in Africa, the Americas and Asia. European traders arrived on the coast of China, attracted by China's unique luxury goods, such as porcelain (giving rise to the English word 'china' for pottery tableware), silk and tea.

The Qing emperors refused to deal with government delegations and were also suspicious of European merchants. But in the late 18th century China opened up the port of Guangzhou (Canton) to limited foreign trade. The Europeans were keen to enlarge this trade – they wanted free access to China, for the work of their Christian missionaries and to sell European manufactured goods. But the Chinese did not want what the Europeans had to offer – they had enough silver and were not interested in European goods. It was only when the British began to exploit the illegal opium trade – which resulted in a series of wars between the two countries (see page 11) – that Western traders won a foothold in China.

Japan

Despite the fact that China and Japan face each other across the East China Sea, and that Japanese culture has been deeply influenced by Chinese culture, the two nations have never been good neighbours. Disputes in the past often centred on the Korean peninsula, which separates them. In the early 20th century, Japan fought with Russia over control of Korea and Manchuria. The conquest and occupation of China by Japan during the Second Sino-Japanese War (1937-45) was brutal; some 20 million Chinese died. This war left deep scars, and many Chinese still feel resentment and distrust towards the Japanese, especially since the Japanese have only recently begun to express some official remorse for what they did.

Stories from the Qing dynasty often depict successful military campaigns – but the dynasty was also threatened by the influence of European traders.

In the Second Sino-Japanese War (1937-45), Japan conquered and occupied most of China.

HUMILIATION

This foreign intrusion on Chinese soil began the 'Century of Humiliation'. Little by little, the Western powers increased their presence in China. With free use of the treaty ports – where foreign laws and taxes applied – their traders, industrialists and Christian missionaries worked throughout China, gradually undermining Chinese traditions, customs and beliefs.

In addition, the emperors were losing power and prestige. Sealed off from the world in the Forbidden City of Beijing, surrounded by complex and ancient rituals, they began to seem too remote and irrelevant to a China that was modernising quickly, and in turmoil.

In 1900, a fierce rebellion against foreigners – led by a secret martial arts society called the 'Boxers' – was suppressed by European, American and Japanese

The 'Chinese diaspora'

There are large communities of Chinese around the world: many Singaporeans are of Chinese origin; the Chinese play a leading role in South-East Asian business; and many live in the 'Chinatowns' of cities such as London, San Francisco and Bangkok.

Large-scale emigration began in the 19th century when Western nations needed cheap labour in their new lands to work in mines and to build railways. Many labourers stayed on, eventually running shops or restaurants. In the 20th century, the civil war and the Communist era saw more Chinese fleeing abroad and today some continue to escape the poverty of rural China, often ending up as illegal immigrants. It is estimated that there are now 35 million Chinese living outside China.

13

troops, and China had to accept more trade concessions and pay compensation. Russia took advantage of the situation to annexe Manchuria, but was pushed out by the Japanese in the Russo-Japanese War of 1904-5.

China was in a state of chaos for most of the first half of the 20th century. In 1908, the Imperial dynasty was thrown into crisis when, on the death of Dowager Empress Cixi, an infant boy called Puyi inherited the throne. He was to be the last emperor of China. In 1911-12, revolutionaries overthrew the Qing dynasty and declared China a republic.

In 1898, Empress Dowager Cixi imprisoned her nephew, Emperor Guangxu, and forced him to give her the power to rule China in his place.

NATIONALISTS AND COMMUNISTS

In 1919, China – now ruled by various warlords who supported the government – was descending into civil war. It was during this period that the Republic's first president, Dr Sun Yat-sen, formed a breakaway republic based around his Nationalist Party, the Kuomintang (KMT).

Inspired by the work of the Russian Communists, who overthrew their government and monarchy in 1917, the Chinese Communist Party (CCP) was founded in 1921. Sun Yat-sen formed a short-lived alliance with the Communists but when he died in 1925 his place was taken by the far more militant Chiang Kai-shek. Under Chiang, the KMT massacred many Communists in an attempt to unify southern China. Surviving Communists – including Mao Zedong, who later became the Communist leader – fled to the countryside, where they were ruthlessly hunted down.

In the 1930s, Japan – the new military power in the East – took advantage of the chaos in China to seize the whole of Manchuria, and later pushed southwards, conquering China's main cities and ports. When Japan attacked the US naval base at Pearl Harbour in the

14

The Chinese Communist Party was inspired by the Russian Communists who showed how power could be given to ordinary peasants and industrial workers.

Hawaiian Islands in 1941, the Pacific War began – but Japan eventually surrendered in 1945 when the US dropped two atomic bombs on Japan. On withdrawal from China, the Japanese left a power vacuum which the Communists and the Nationalists raced to fill. The civil war now resumed with even greater ferocity.

The communist 'Red Army' was better organised and more popular than the Nationalists, who were corrupt and poorly equipped. Eventually the Communists triumphed in 1949 and the Nationalists were forced to retreat to the island of Taiwan. The era of Mao's Communist China – now renamed the People's Republic of China (PRC) – had begun. The PRC was recognised by the Soviet Union, Britain and other nations. The USA, however, continued to recognise the Nationalists in Taiwan as the legitimate government of China.

The Long March

In October 1934, the Communists found themselves trapped in Jiangxi province. Around 100,000 broke free and a year later, after travelling more than 9,000 km, and fighting KMT forces along the way, they reached Shaanxi province. Only about 8,000 survived. The Long March remains one of the great heroic tales of communism – many veterans became leading figures of the Communist Party, including Mao Zedong and Deng Xiaoping.

COMMUNIST CHINA

China became a communist country in 1949, and is now the only major country in the world ruled by a communist regime. China has gone through many changes since 1949, ranging from a totalitarian state during the Cultural Revolution to the more flexible and open China that we know today.

Mao Zedong believed that he could create an entirely new kind of Chinese society by turning traditions on their head. Under his rule, many millions of Chinese people died as a direct result of government policy. Yet Mao is still revered today. This has much to do with the fact that he brought the 'Century of Humiliation' to a close and laid the foundations of a new 'modern' China.

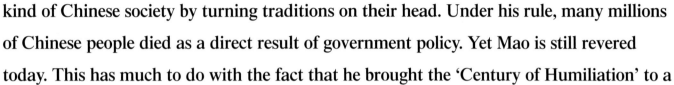

Wherever you go in China, tributes to Mao are never far away. Statues line the streets, buildings are adorned with his image and his picture appears in pamphlets, posters and tourist souvenirs.

BEHIND CLOSED DOORS

When Mao Zedong became China's leader in 1949, he had numerous problems to confront. After decades of war, the Chinese economy was in tatters, and the nation was still deeply divided. The first task was to shore up communist power and create stability. Mao did this by eliminating opposition. Anyone found opposing the new regime (in public or in private) was arrested, sent to a labour camp to be 're-educated' or at worst, killed. No one was exempt from the finger of suspicion and many thousands of people died for their beliefs in the first five years of communist rule.

This was the era of the Cold War, when the 'free' West opposed the communist East. Initially China had a close relationship with Russia and appeared to be a threat to the West. But by 1949, China had sealed itself off from the world. Only later, in the 1970s, did news emerge of quite what had been going on.

THE GREAT CAMPAIGNS

China's ordinary people – the peasants and factory workers – had suffered greatly from the inequalities of Imperial China and Nationalist and Japanese rule. Now, in principle, they stood to benefit from a communist government that would look after them, with better schools, housing, healthcare and the promise of permanent jobs and enough food to eat.

This presented an immense challenge for the government. To achieve it, Mao demanded discipline, and the Chinese Communist Party (CCP) ruled with an iron rod. A hierarchy of government officers helped to impose an authoritarian regime – the press was strictly censored and all members of society were called upon to act as loyal revolutionaries serving, for instance, in the People's Militias. Even children were expected to chant revolutionary songs at school.

All property now belonged to the State; farmland was reorganised into huge state-run 'collective farms' and industries were nationalised. Factory workers and peasant farmers had to produce goods in accordance with State-set targets. No one could earn extra money by trading or setting up their own business – everything was geared to the good of the people, which meant the State.

The CCP produced grand plans to shape the future, usually under the heading of a slogan. One major campaign – called the 'Great Leap Forward' – began in 1957. This was designed to rapidly convert China into a major industrial power by accelerating collectivisation and growth. Society was reorganised into huge working communes, causing widespread disruption to family life. The People's Liberation Army (PLA) suppressed any opposition.

Deng Xiaoping

Deng Xiaoping (1904-97) was a dedicated communist who took part in the Long March. He rose to power as deputy premier under Zhou Enlai in 1973, when he tried to move China towards moderate economic reform. Radical supporters of the Cultural Revolution persuaded Mao that these reforms would unravel all the achievements of Mao's communism, and Deng was ousted in April 1976. But after Mao's death that September, the moderates won their struggle against the radicals, and Deng was reinstated. Although he did not hold a high-profile post, Deng was the power behind successive premiers Hua Guofeng and Zhao Ziyang. Deng's main aims were to push ahead with economic modernisation, and to improve relations with Western nations, a process that he set in motion in 1978. He remained a major influence in China, and the chief architect of its modernisation, virtually until his death, aged 92.

During the 1970s, Mao agreed to a series of table tennis matches between Chinese and US teams, helping to improve international relations.

The Great Leap Forward was a disaster. Agriculture was neglected and the conversion to industry was carried out too quickly. The result was the greatest man-made famine in history. After three crop failures in 1959-61, some 14-20 million people starved to death. Meanwhile, the CCP blamed the weather.

In 1966, Mao introduced the 'Cultural Revolution', designed to shake up Chinese society. City-dwellers were sent to work in the countryside; colleges and universities were closed; and leading members of the CCP were removed from office. It was, in part, a crude power struggle, designed by Mao to eradicate his more moderate rivals. The Revolution officially ended in 1969 when the PLA restored order, but the effects lived on and, thanks to propaganda tactics, Mao's status was given a significant boost.

Mao Zedong

Mao Zedong (1893-1976) was one of the colossal figures of 20th-century history. He ruled China for nearly three decades, riding a rollercoaster of revolutionary change. He was adored by millions, abroad as well as in China; his book of wisdom called 'The Thoughts of Chairman Mao' (nicknamed 'The Little Red Book') was distributed across China and around the world in the late 1960s. 900 million copies have now been produced, making this the second most-printed book ever (after the Bible).

Mao was the son of prosperous peasants from Shaoshan, in Hunan province. He trained and worked as a teacher, where he came into contact with Western ideas, and the communist ideas of Karl Marx. In 1921, Mao was a founding member of the CCP and later emerged as leader during the Long March of 1934-5. Hard-working and charismatic, Mao was driven by his vision of a harmonious, classless, powerful and united China. But in his haste to achieve this, he introduced social and economic experiments that proved disastrous.

Mao resigned as chairman of the PRC after the Great Leap Forward, but remained chairman of the Central Committee of the Chinese Communist Party, and effective head of state. He was made Supreme Commander of China in 1970, and retained a decisive grip on power until his death at the age of 82.

17

Tienanmen Square is dominated by Mao's tomb – a fitting reminder of the great leader who died in 1976.

INTERNATIONAL RELATIONS

At the start of the Cold War, the West feared that China might form an alliance with the Soviet Union (USSR). Both nations had a close relationship with the Communist regime of North Korea. During the Korean War (1950-53), United Nations forces led by the US came to the defence of South Korea, pushing into North Korea, almost as far as the Chinese border. With Soviet military backing, China intervened to save North Korea from defeat, and fought on until the war ended in stalemate.

Such events did not endear China to the Western world. Nor did its two conflicts with India during the 1960s. China and the USSR were also supporters of Communist North Vietnam, during the Vietnam War (1959-75). In 1979, China's relations with Vietnam deteriorated when China invaded northern Vietnam in order to force it to withdraw from Cambodia, where it had overthrown the savage, Chinese-backed Communist regime of Pol Pot. This was the last time the Chinese army was used in a major international conflict.

To the West's relief, fears of a China-USSR alliance proved unfounded. When Stalin, the Soviet leader, died in 1956, the USSR adopted a less rigid form of communism, and began to show greater willingness to negotiate with the West. Mao made it known that he profoundly disagreed with this policy. As the disaster of the Great Leap Forward unfolded, the USSR withdrew its advisors from China, and by 1960 the rift was complete. Both countries massed troops along the border in Xinjiang and Manchuria, coming close to all-out war.

Tienanmen Square

In the 1980s, communism across the world came under great pressure. The Soviet Union (under President Mikhail Gorbachev) had begun to introduce democratic reforms; Eastern Europe had begun to liberate itself from communism. Was it now the turn of China? Tensions in China had been building up over several years, but the biggest and most visible rebellion began on 4 May 1989 when one million students and workers gathered in Tienanmen Square to call for democratic reform. For a time it seemed that the Chinese Communist Party might be swayed but after a month-long protest, government leaders (including Deng Xiaoping) could no longer tolerate the revolt. On 4 June, the army intervened.

No one knows how many of the protesters were killed – the official number is 200, but the death-toll is suspected to be far higher. Many protesters are in prison, while others are still missing. News of the violent end to the revolt spread rapidly around the world. Many countries complained about China's violation of human rights and broke off economic and diplomatic relations. But such humanitarian concerns were soon brushed aside as China's prosperity resumed, and the rest of the world wanted to have a part of it.

During the 1970s, US president Richard Nixon successfully opened up diplomatic relations with China.

NIXON IN CHINA

The Vietnam War was the USA's most bruising direct conflict with communism – costing the lives of 57,000 Americans and more than 2 million Vietnamese. However, at the height of the war, US president Richard Nixon attempted to improve relations with China, in order to tip the balance against the USSR in the ongoing Cold War conflict. China's contacts with the outside world were so few that Nixon had to employ unorthodox means to open discussions. In 1971, he arranged for the USA to play the Chinese at table tennis. This so-called 'ping-pong diplomacy' was enough to secure a high-level meeting with the Chinese government. That same year, China joined the United Nations (UN) – evidence that China wanted to take a more active role in world affairs. In 1972, Nixon met with Mao Zedong and prime minister Zhou Enlai. It was the first time Communist China had received such a high level visit from the Western world, and it opened the doors, just a touch, to change.

Hong Kong

In 1842, China was forced to give the small island of Hong Kong to the British as part of the Treaty of Nanking in the aftermath of the First Opium War. In 1898, the British also took a 99-year lease on a chunk of land on the mainland (called the New Territories) to supply their new island colony with farm produce and water. Soon British firms and Chinese residents made Hong Kong into a great trading port and, after the Second World War, into one of the world's leading financial centres. But Hong Kong could not survive without the support of the New Territories, whose lease expired in 1997. In the 1980s, the British government began negotiations to return Hong Kong to China. It was a delicate matter: China was delighted to gain a major financial centre but many of the Hong Kong Chinese did not take gladly to joining a communist country with a reputation for economic mismanagement. However, since Britain's departure in June 1997, the CCP has allowed Hong Kong some freedom to manage its own affairs, and it has remained a vibrant financial centre.

19

FROM MAO TO DENG

When Mao died in 1976, there was a brief power struggle in the Chinese Communist Party. Supporters of the Cultural Revolution tried to cling onto power but, instead, the moderate Deng Xiaoping won through. By the time of Mao's death, China could at least claim that it had found a way to produce enough food for its citizens. But China was 30 years behind in terms of technology and the standards of living enjoyed by many Western nations. If China was to progress, something had to change. In 1978, Deng Xiaoping oversaw this change by recommending that the CCP loosen State controls on the economy.

Communism opposes capitalism – the economic system of the West. Under communism, the State controls everything, but under capitalism, a 'free market economy' allows people to do what they want with their money and their jobs. Deng Xiaoping's policies allowed a limited amount of capitalism to enter the communist economy. At first this had only a minor impact across China but by opening its doors to foreign trade, China was able to export cheap products and to win investment in new factories from foreign companies attracted by China's low labour costs. And so China's industries began a process of rapid modernisation.

Can China become a democracy?

During the Tienanmen Square episode in 1989, the outside world wondered if China might be on the brink of democracy. To all those whose believe in the benefits of democracy, and the freedoms and humanitarian advantages that go with it, it seemed like a wonderful prospect. But it was also a frightening one. Could China transform itself into a democracy without sliding into chaos? China has a history of highly centralised authoritarian rule. From the first dynasty of emperors to the rule of Mao Zedong, China has never experienced a representative democracy – where the people have a right to choose who rules them. But perhaps this is neither appropriate nor desirable? This could certainly present a difficult challenge in modern China, with its population of 1.3 billion: if the Chinese had a parliament with 1,000 MPs, each would represent 1.3 million constituents. But it is not impossible – India (with a population of 1 billion) manages to elect a parliament with 550 members. But others think that China would find it easier to move towards a different kind of democracy, in which the voice of the people can be represented through their communities, rather than on the basis of one-person, one-vote elections.

Despite notable improvements in its food production, during the 1970s China was 30 years behind the Western world in terms of technology and standards of living.

THE QUEST FOR DEMOCRACY

Many of the Chinese, especially the young, hoped
that these economic changes would be accompanied
by political changes, and that China would move
towards greater democracy. This, however, was not
the intention of the CCP, which has firmly held onto
power. China remains a one-party state, whose
officials are appointed, not elected by a public vote.

The years leading up to 1989 saw a period, overseen
by Deng Xiaoping, when restrictions on debate and
discussion were eased; but this coincided with a
downward turn in the economy that led to price-
inflation, unemployment and discontent. When the
international community restricted trade after the
Tienanmen Square massacre, China's economic and
political reforms came to a halt and CCP leaders who
were sympathetic to reform were purged. One of the
new leaders to emerge at this stage was Jiang Zemin,
who became president in 1993. That same year, Deng
Xiaoping gave the signal for the resumption of the
reforms, proclaiming the development of a 'socialist
market economy'. Now the boom really took off.

By the time of Mao's death,
China had recovered from the
great famines of the early
1960s. In death, Mao has
continued to be revered for
helping to set China on the
road to modernisation.

Today, China's 'socialist market
economy' has seen the introduction
of many Western influences. It is
now quite usual to see a Starbucks
or an Ikea in the cities of China.

21

WORKSHOP OF THE WORLD

The achievement of China's economic development over the last 25 years has been phenomenal. Today, China's production includes 33 per cent of the world's computers, 40 per cent of the world's colour televisions and 66 per cent of microwave ovens. Most toys in Western shops now have 'Made in China' stamped on them. Behind this success story lies a powerful ambition, felt right through Chinese society, to modernise and get rich – or at least richer. The Chinese want to improve their daily lives, to realise their potential in business, industry, art and design, and to share in the advantages of modern life, like other people in successful nations. They want a better world, better standards of living, better education, and greater opportunities for their children.

WINNING WAYS

One of China's greatest assets is its huge (and cheap) workforce. Wages of less than US $1 per hour means that the cost of manufacturing is also low, making Chinese products very attractive abroad.

China's economy is mainly export-driven. Some companies produce purely Chinese products, but others manufacture cheap products that have been initially designed and developed by foreign companies abroad. Two-thirds of China's exports are now products made for foreign companies.

China has been very successful in attracting major foreign companies who put money into building factories and developing their businesses in China – of the 500 top multinational companies in the world, 400 have set up businesses in China. In the late 1970s, the Chinese government deliberately set out to achieve this by developing Special Economic Zones (SEZs) – coastal cities with large, new industrial parks specifically designed as places where foreign investors could build factories, and could enjoy special advantages, such as low taxation.

Fifty per cent of the world's clothes are now made in China – where labour and production costs are cheap.

TECHNOLOGICAL SHIFT

Foreign companies did not simply bring jobs for millions of Chinese factory workers. They also brought technology and know-how. Twenty years ago 'Made in China' was found mainly on low-tech products, such as clothes, plastic toys and cheap steel tools. Very quickly China has learnt to produce high-tech products, such as televisions, mobile phones, computers, software and modern medicines. Increasingly, China is also designing and developing these products too.

Many of the old and inefficient state-owned enterprises (SOEs), producing products like steel, railway engines and industrial machinery, have been closed down or sold off in favour of lighter industries that benefit from cheap labour. But China has not turned its back on heavy industry entirely. It has retained and modernised certain major industries, such as shipbuilding and car manufacture. One major prestige project is the Maglev, Shanghai's magnetic-levitation train, which travels to and from Shanghai's international airport at speeds of up to 430 km per hour.

Some 50 million people now live in a cluster of Special Economic Zones – Shenzhen (above), Zhuhai and Shantou – in the Pearl River Delta, near Guangzhou and Hong Kong.

Communism and wealth

In 2001, the Chinese Communist Party announced a major shift in its policy: it would allow people in business to become members of the Party. Under the 'Three Represents' scheme introduced by President Jiang Zemin, the CCP would welcome business people into its fold.

Communism was designed to benefit all the people, not just the few. It was capitalism – the enemy of communism – that allowed people the freedom to get rich, and so permitting the divide between the rich few and the many poor.

The Chinese Communist Party, however, was taking a practical approach. By introducing a controlled form of capitalism, it would allow some people to become wealthy, in order to lead the way and to help the less well-off to follow in their tracks. Now a quarter of the names on the list of China's richest people are members of the Party.

The Maglev train-link to Shanghai's airport opened in 2004.

23

NATURAL RESOURCES

To feed its new growth, China has needed a colossal increase in natural resources. Fortunately, China is relatively rich in many of these as the world's leading producer of coal, aluminium and zinc and as an exporter of other minerals such as tungsten, tin and magnesium.

China stands fifth in the world oil production – with reserves found mainly in the far west, around the city of Ürümqi, and off the eastern coast – but it still has to import a third of what it uses. China's building boom also consumes 40 per cent of the world's concrete, and 27 per cent of the world's steel. China's thirst for natural resources is having a major impact on world markets. The prices of steel, copper and oil have risen sharply as a result of China's demand – which is good for producing countries but bad for those who have to buy resources for their industries. In its search for natural resources, China has now set up numerous companies abroad. China has been mining in Australia, the USA and Peru, and drilling for oil in Venezuela and Sudan.

Although China's oil industry produces a fifth of the world's oil supplies, its rapid industrialisation and building boom mean that China still has to import a third of the oil that it uses.

 **Should Western architects be rushing to design prestige buildings for the Chinese government?**

In September and October 2004, Beijing hosted a large international architecture fair attracting many of the world's leading architects. China is currently one of the most exciting countries for modern architecture. Many of the big cities are undertaking huge building projects, with innovative designs to demonstrate that China is a modern up-to-the-minute state. One example is the 'National Swimming Centre' in Beijing (right) designed by Australian-based architects PTW and engineering firm Ove Arup. More controversial is the extraordinary new 'Z-Crisscross' building for China Central Television (CCTV) in Beijing, by the Dutch architect Rem Koolhaas, and Ove Arup, to be completed in 2008. The rush to design prestige buildings for China has attracted some criticism; China, after all, is not a democratic country, and has a poor record in human rights. China Central Television is the heavily censored tool of Chinese government propaganda. Should a Western architect be so keen to design a prestige building to house it?

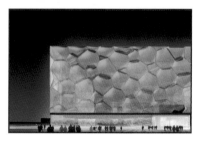

Pudong financial district, Shanghai: since the early 1990s, the skylines of many of the most prosperous industrial cities have been transformed by sparkling new skyscrapers.

REAPING THE REWARDS

The benefits of China's industrial boom can best be seen in the cities. Shanghai's skyline will soon include a World Financial Centre (over 460 metres tall) and Guangzhou has plans for a television tower rising to 600 metres, the world's tallest structure.

In the past, property was owned by the State but today some 70 per cent of homes in Shanghai are privately owned. Car ownership has also risen massively – some two million new cars were sold in China in 2003, up 80 per cent on the previous year.

During Mao's era, all the Chinese dressed in blue worksuits and rode bicycles. Now, looking good has become an obsession among many young city-dwellers, prompted by an explosion in advertising. These developments reflect the new wealth of a large number of Chinese citizens. City-dwellers have become enthusiastic supporters of the 'consumer society', helping to fuel new enterprises that cater for the domestic market. Leisure, for

instance, has become a massive growth industry with new cinemas, internet cafés, bowling alleys and ski resorts. Some of the Chinese have become very rich indeed. They can live in luxury apartments, take holidays abroad and educate their children in private schools overseas.

Chinese shopping malls now contain fashionable boutiques, electronic gadget shops and fast-food restaurants.

25

The Shanghai International Circuit – host of the first Chinese Grand Prix in 2004 – is now the most challenging Formula 1 track in the world. The grandstand accommodates over 200,000 spectators.

NATIONAL PRESTIGE

The Chinese government is basking in the reflected glory of its recent achievements. It is keen to promote China as a modern, successful and prosperous state – one that does not just imitate the modern Western world, but has something unique to contribute to it.

China already enjoys the international publicity attracted by some of its most impressive building projects. But it also sees important advantages in mounting, participating in – and even winning – major international sporting events. Beijing 2008 is already set to be a successful venture, following China's form in recent Olympics – China came fourth in the medals league in Atlanta 1996, third in Sydney 2000 and second in Athens 2004. Similarly, China invested considerable money and effort in its national football team for the World Cup of 2002, employing the Serb coach Bora Milutinovic. China also spent an estimated £133 million on international motor-racing when it staged the Shanghai Grand Prix of 2004 – China's first ever Grand Prix.

In 2003 and 2004, China played host to the Miss World Contest, watched by millions of television viewers around the world. China has also recently attracted international music performers for televised concerts at historic sites across the country. In September 2004, American R&B star Alicia Keys performed at the first foreign concert staged at the Great Wall near Beijing. A month later, Jean-Michel Jarre played at the Forbidden City – the first outdoor concert in the world to use 5.1 Dolby Digital Surround sound (previously only used in cinemas).

None of these achievements would have been possible without the wholehearted support of the Chinese people – as the statistics show. The Shanghai Grand Prix was the best-attended Grand Prix of the entire 2004 season; and the Alicia Keys concert was a sell-out, even though the cheapest tickets cost 100 yuan (£6) – the equivalent of three days' pay for many workers – and the top-priced tickets cost 10,000 yuan. For the first time in many years, the Chinese people are able to afford the ways of the West – and they are intent on having a good time.

STRESSES AND STRAINS

Not everyone in China is benefiting from the economic boom. While the wealthy minority tend to live in the coastal cities of the east, the vast majority live in deprived rural areas inland. The rural population earn around one-third of city wages. Many men and women leave their homes and families in the hope of earning a decent living in the city – only to find that the wages are low and the living conditions wretched. The poor feel let down by the Chinese Communist Party which they used to trust to protect them. The CCP continues to offer the hope that the economic boom will make things better for everyone. But there is some doubt that the economic boom can be sustained.

PEOPLE ON THE MOVE

The world's greatest ever migration is taking place in China. Over the past two decades, around 200 million Chinese have left their homes in the countryside to head for the cities, hoping to find work and a better standard of living. Many are disappointed. In the cities, factory-workers can earn as little as £2 a day (working up to 11 hours a day, six days a week). The work is usually tedious or physically demanding. Safety standards are often so low as to be dangerous – well below international standards.

Many workers try to save as much money as they can to support their families back home. This means that they can only afford to live in basic hostels, where they sleep in dormitories. These workers cannot be a part of the consumer boom that is on display in the new shopping malls in the city centres: they cannot afford it, nor – as migrant workers – are they made to feel welcome.

The attraction of work in the cities is leading to a mass migration in China. But dreams are rarely fulfilled and the poverty trap remains.

URBAN SPRAWL

Meanwhile, it is not always easy for those who have always lived in the cities. The building boom has turned many cities into huge building sites. Traditional houses – although thought to be small and unsanitary, with dirty alleys and shared toilets – have always created a close sense of community which many Chinese have enjoyed. Now, they are being replaced by surging tower blocks. In the big cities, like Beijing, many old communities have been uprooted and swept away. Resistance has been met with fierce opposition from property developers and accommodation nearby is seldom an option – it is simply too expensive. Instead, residents are forced to move to flats in the suburbs with no sense of community at all.

STRAINS ON THE SYSTEM

China's roads are also set to get busier. One of the great ambitions now of the Chinese is to own a car. Although there is currently only one car owner for every 150 people, if this figure were to approach the ways of the US (with two cars per household) there could be up to 650 million cars in China – more cars than the rest of the world put together! The implications of this for traffic management and pollution is causing great concern. Meanwhile, China has been building roads furiously – enough tarmac over the last ten years to go around the equator sixteen times.

China's infrastructure provision – roads, railways, aircraft, ships, communications systems

The Three Gorges Dam

With its unchallenged control of the government, the Chinese Communist Party (CCP) is able to undertake and organise vast projects, on a scale that is impossible to contemplate in most other countries. The Three Gorges Dam on the Yangtze River is the world's largest engineering project, and will be the world's biggest hydroelectric power station. It is being built to provide power to central and eastern China, but also to prevent the Yangtze River from causing the floods that regularly devastate the lower reaches of the valley.

But the project has been surrounded in controversy from the start. The Three Gorges formed a scenic stretch of river,

steeped in history, which will be destroyed by the reservoir formed by the dam. In addition, more than one million residents of the Gorge have had to be moved. Environmentalists believe that the dam, and its huge 640-km-long reservoir, will alter the climate of the region and will prevent the natural flow of rich silt from fertilising the fields downstream – forcing farmers to use damaging chemical fertilisers instead. And if the dam ever broke, a massive catastrophe would occur. But the CCP has gone ahead nonetheless. The project is due for completion in 2008.

and power supplies – is inadequate at present. The economic boom has made the situation worse by outstripping China's ability to provide basic services. China's cities and factories frequently suffer from power shortages. Although coal is mainly used for generating electricity, China is now looking at the possibilities of hydroelectric power – such as the new Three Gorges Dam on the Yangtze River. But hydroelectric power only provides 18 per cent of China's power needs. China has nine nuclear reactors, but again these only provide 2 per cent of China's electricity requirements.

CRISIS IN THE COUNTRYSIDE

Even more pressing are China's problems in the countryside. Two-thirds of China's workforce live in rural areas and farming is a major industry. Farming is an essential part of China's economy – as exports, but also to feed the Chinese themselves. Farm production has risen massively in recent years but farmers find it increasingly difficult to make a profit. This is partly because local governments now raise

With the demise of state-run farms, farmers now work under contract to local authorities, selling excess produce for private gain.

their income through tax, and through profits from farming and industry. Many rural communities complain that tax rates are too high, government officials are corrupt, and that standards of safety and healthcare are being sacrificed in the interest of profit. All these factors have led to a feeling of great frustration in rural areas – triggering a series of violent disturbances and riots.

29

Is China's growth set to continue?

Here are some of the fears that China's economy may not be quite as strong as it seems:
• China could be vulnerable to the natural world business cycle: if global demand slows down, the Chinese economy could go down with a bump.
• The Chinese economy could be in danger of producing more than the market can bear. However, economic measures have curbed the growth rate to 7 per cent.
• If China's colossal growth rate can't be sustained, it may suffer from social conflict as the poor begin to despair.
• With loans of around £370 billion (that are unlikely to be paid back) China's government-owned banks may fail.

• Foreign countries may introduce import taxes to protect their manufacturers from cheap competition in China.
• Demands for greater democracy may undermine the CCP's grip on power and result in political turmoil.
• If labour costs rise, China may lose its competitive edge and foreign businesses will look elsewhere.
• Despite its efforts to modernise its business practices, foreign companies complain of a lack of transparency in contracts, and corruption. Piracy also remains a problem.

That said, the general view is that the underlying trends favour China's continued growth in the long term.

DEAF EARS

One of the problems with the Chinese political system is that there is no one to complain to. The Chinese Communist Party has never been open to criticism and, nowadays, government officials are tempted to protect their businesses and profits rather than the people who work for them. Workers, for example, who complain that they are exposed to toxic chemicals that damage their health are unlikely to have their complaint addressed. At the heart of the problem is the one-party state, which does not permit opposition parties. The only way that ordinary people can hope to make their complaints heard is to dress them up as constructive suggestions for change. They can join official pressure groups and non-governmental organisations (NGOs), and work within the system, but these are subject to the whims of the CCP, which may suddenly refuse to tolerate an NGO and close it down without warning.

CENSORSHIP

The CCP has three methods of keeping criticism at bay: censorship, propaganda and the suppression of persistent critics. The government controls all the media (e.g. newspapers, radio and television) and prevents the publishing or broadcasting of information that it judges harmful to the State. The government also censors use of the internet – jokingly referred to as the 'Great Firewall of China'.

The recent development of commercial radio stations now offers a wider range of subject matter than ever before – such as talk shows and Western music. However, news items still follow the government line, being broadcast from Beijing through China Radio International. China is now also more open to foreign media. That said, foreign media-owners know the restrictions that operate in China, and tend to play by the rules in order to maintain their business interests there: they are in China to make a profit, not to rock the boat.

Strangers in their own land

A colossal number of migrant rural workers now live in the eastern boom-cities and industrial zones – perhaps 130 million of them (more than twice the entire population of Britain). In these cities, migrant workers are treated like foreigners, even if they come from the neighbouring province. They do not enjoy the same rights as the native city-dwellers – such as rights to education, pensions or welfare. Every year they have to apply for, and pay for, a new residence permit, which effectively makes them second-class citizens. They can qualify to apply to be a permanent resident of their adopted city only after staying there, and working continuously, for some seven years (and in some cities, never). Many migrant workers have

been driven to despair, even suicide, by their poor wages (or the failure of their employers to pay them at all), their miserable working conditions and their low status.

BURYING THE TRUTH

With its control over the media, the Chinese government is able to present China in the best possible light to its people. But this also means that it can hide uncomfortable truths. Recently, China has had to come to terms with the fact that it is facing an AIDS crisis. The United Nations has estimated that China will have 10 million AIDS victims by 2010 – one of the highest growth rates in the world. China has only recently acknowledged that it needs to address the problem with a public health campaign.

If the government feels that someone has overstepped the mark by expressing criticism and dissent, it can act with brutal severity. Dissidents (persistent critics) may be arrested and sentenced to many years in prison. The human rights group Amnesty International says there are currently tens of thousands of political prisoners in China; many of them are held in the world's largest network of labour camps. The Chinese government also ruthlessly punishes crime: it is believed that more than 700 people are executed every year, many of them publicly.

Minorities and dissidents

The Chinese government has been particularly criticised abroad for its treatment of minority groups within its borders. Although Chinese culture is a product of many faiths, the Chinese government does not encourage any form of religion. It has tried to limit the influence of Christianity and Islam, and has taken a particularly strong dislike to the Falun Gong ('Buddhist Law'), a religious sect that encourages meditation and exercise. Since the events of Tienanmen Square in 1989, the CCP has discouraged large gatherings – something which the Falun Gong's popularity made possible. In 1999, the government broke up a gathering of 10,000 Falun Gong followers in Beijing during the Spring Festival. Two months later the government banned the Falun Gong altogether.

Critics abroad have also been incensed by China's treatment of Tibetans – one of 57 non-Chinese ethnic groups in China, who make up about 8 per cent of the total population. China has tried to stamp out Tibetan Buddhist culture since the days of the Cultural Revolution. Other minority groups, like the Uighurs (Muslims living in the remote region of Xinjiang) complain that they feel like second-class citizens in their own land. This resentment has led to a campaign of terrorism against the Chinese.

31

In 1999, the Falun Gong had over 100 million followers. The religious group preaches a way of achieving spiritual purification through meditation and exercise.

LETTING THE PEOPLE DOWN

Although criticism is difficult in China, it is clear that many citizens are beginning to feel disillusioned with the CCP. They consider that the deal it has struck with the business world favours business ahead of the needs of ordinary people. In the past, state-run industries provided workers with jobs, pensions, healthcare, and even housing. People were more likely to accept government repression because they knew that their interests were being looked after. But now they are not so sure – they complain of corruption among Party officials, a decline in the provision of healthcare and a reduction in school funding. Many Chinese are fleeing abroad – in despair of ever lifting themselves out of poverty in China. Assisted by human-traffickers, they travel illegally to countries where they hope to find a better life. But as illegal immigrants, they are vulnerable to exploitation. In 2004, 21 Chinese people, employed as cockle-pickers, drowned in Morecambe Bay, Lancashire, in the UK, as a direct result of this kind of exploitation.

The SARS crisis

Severe Acute Respiratory Syndrome (SARS), a type of pneumonia, is a new killer disease that began in southern China in November 2002. The Chinese government initially tried to cover up the outbreak, and then to play down its significance – all of which allowed the disease to spread, both in China and abroad. Only in February 2003 did China officially acknowledge the problem and inform the World Health Organisation. By June 2003, 775 people had died. The scare lasted until the last cases of SARS were cleared and released from hospital in May 2004. Throughout much of this time, China was under quarantine and travel within China, and to-and-from China, was severely restricted. The Chinese tourist industry was badly damaged, as too was business. SARS threatened to seriously dent China's economy.

The SARS crisis of 2003 was an embarrassing episode for the Chinese government, and it learnt some important lessons. The crisis demonstrated clearly how China's tendency towards secrecy could be counterproductive, and how greater openness would serve it better.

PUTTING UP WITH IT

That said, many people in China have great hope for the future. Those who are enjoying the benefits of the economic boom feel that they have their leaders to thank for it. If the CCP can continue to deliver prosperity, they are not going to complain.

The Chinese government may be authoritarian and secretive but it is more flexible now than it was in the past. Generally, people in China feel freer to express their opinions today. Most users of the internet are not searching for criticism against the government; they are looking at advertisements and product announcements, fact-based information, or playing the latest online computer games.

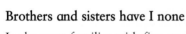

Brothers and sisters have I none

In the past, families with five or six children were common in China. By the 1970s, however, the spiralling increase in China's already huge population looked unsustainable – soon China would not be able to feed itself and the Communist revolution would be crushed by numbers. In 1979, the government introduced a law stating that married couples could only have one child.

This policy is now into its second generation. For most children in China today, their family consists of just parents and grandparents. Some are horribly spoilt, and have been termed 'Little Emperors'. They may show a tendency to be selfish, to find it hard to share, or to make friends. Meanwhile, children complain of being under unbearable pressure from their elders to succeed in school, having to spend their days and evenings studying from an early age.

One side effect of the policy is that parents have less offspring to support them in old age. Also, there are now more boys than girls in China. Chinese parents have traditionally preferred boys and some choose to terminate a pregnancy if they know they are expecting a girl. As a result of this imbalance, girls are in great demand when it comes to dating!

The environment

Of the 20 most polluted cities in the world, 16 are in China. This single fact demonstrates the scale of the environmental problems facing China. And with rapid industrial development, and an increase in car use, the situation is set to get worse:

• Some 80 per cent of China's electricity is generated by burning high-sulphur coal, a major source of air pollution.

• All the major rivers – a source of drinking water in many cities – are dangerously polluted by industrial waste, sewage and chemical fertiliser waste from fields.

• Deforestation has caused massive soil erosion, and flooding because rainwater runs off the bare soil. Logging has also caused the Gobi desert to spread to within 250 km of Beijing, with the result that the capital now frequently suffers from dust storms.

The good news is that China is actively trying to address these problems. The issue should also be kept in perspective: the USA's carbon dioxide (greenhouse gas) emissions amount to 19.8 tonnes per person; the figure for China is 2.5 tonnes per person. But China has four times as many people, and its emission rate is rising rapidly.

33

INTERNATIONAL RELATIONS

Now that China has become a player on the world stage, activities in China are of global importance. In the past, China has been treated with some caution – as a secretive and unpredictable participant with values that were often hard to comprehend. Now foreign countries have made special efforts to understand China and to sympathise with it. China is keen to cement international relations and is careful to play even-handedly with all parties. It cannot afford to offend trading partners while its economic success remains fragile and precious, but it is also determined to conduct relations in its own unique way.

Chinese president Hu Jintao waves during the Asia-Pacific Economic Cooperation Summit in Santiago, Chile, November 2004.

The question of Taiwan

Taiwan is an island about the size of Switzerland, located 150 km off the coast of mainland China (the PRC). After the Nationalists retreated here in 1949, Taiwan developed as a democracy with a capitalist economy and became highly successful. The PRC has always claimed Taiwan as its territory, viewing it as a kind of rebel province. The Chinese could be provoked into invading if Taiwan ever declared itself independent, but this looks unlikely because:

• The PRC probably doesn't have the military strength to conquer a Taiwan supported by the USA.

• The PRC would rather avoid international outrage.

• Taiwan is one of the PRC's main trading partners.

• The political systems of Taiwan and the PRC may become similar, encouraging a possible reunification.

REGIONAL POLITICS

China's first concerns are with its neighbours – Japan, South Korea and Taiwan rank among China's leading partners in trade. China's important trading relationship with Japan has helped to smooth over some of the deep scars left by its history of conflict in the 20th century. China also has mutually profitable relations with the Association of South-East Asian Nations (ASEAN), which brings together ten countries. Before the slump of 1997, several of these countries were known as the 'Asian Tigers', because of their rapid rise to prosperity. They still have the potential to develop further – and quickly. In 2001, China, Japan and Korea linked up with ASEAN to form ASEAN + 3. One day this could evolve into a powerful trading bloc, acting as a counterweight to the US and the European Union (EU).

China faces two tricky issues in East Asia: North Korea and Taiwan. North Korea is a staunchly communist country, desperately poor, and geared to a cultish following of its leader, Kim Jong Il. Recently North Korea was propelled to the top of the international agenda through its renewed desire to own nuclear weapons, causing alarm in the international community (particularly Japan and the US). China has been an ally to North Korea, although the relationship is tainted by mutual suspicion, fuelled by the fact that in 1992 China established full trade and diplomatic relations with South Korea,

North Korea's sworn enemy. China therefore plays a pivotal role in the Six-Party Talks (involving North Korea, South Korea, China, USA, Russia and Japan) designed to resolve the North Korean nuclear ambitions peacefully. Another flashpoint is Taiwan which China considers belongs to them, and on certain occasions has threatened to invade. This would trigger a major international conflict, but – for the time being at least – is considered unlikely.

The Chinese army – the People's Liberation Army (PLA) – is essentially the Communist Party's army with political and family connections dominating the higher ranks and a soldier base consisting of mainly rural peasants. However, a modernisation process is under way.

Should the international community make an issue of China's human rights record?

At the news of the Tienanmen Square massacre the world was outraged and many countries vowed not to deal with China while it treated its citizens so badly. Since then, China's human rights record has not noticeably improved, but China's booming economy has encouraged the world to turn more of a blind eye.

Those that favour this policy argue that:
• The Chinese government is sensitive to criticism, so criticising China's human rights record would harm trade.
• Human rights are China's own problem, and it is wrong to meddle in China's internal affairs.

• By trading with China, countries can help to push China along the path to greater openness and democracy.

Critics argue that:
• Trade with China encourages the Chinese government to believe it can get away with abusing human rights.
• Western democratic countries are being hypocritical if, on the one hand, they claim to promote democracy and human rights, and, on the other, they trade with China, without making this an issue.
• By ignoring China's human rights record, we are letting down the Chinese people who are fighting for change.

THE SUPERPOWER ACROSS THE SEA

China's relationship with the US is complex. During the Cold War, the US developed a basic understanding with China, as a way of building up pressure on the Soviet Union. Then, from 1978, the US became China's largest trading partner. This is partly due to the fact that the Chinese renminbi is pegged to the US dollar at an artificially low rate of exchange – making Chinese goods even cheaper and more attractive to the US and other world traders. But the arrival of cheap Chinese goods has devastated many of America's industries, such as clothes manufacturing.

Because the US dollar is the main world currency, China is pouring money into the US by buying government bonds. This has the effect of supporting the US's huge trade deficit. Some observers believe this is a dangerous situation: the US economy is now financially dependent on China, which holds billions of dollars in US government bonds and its foreign exchange reserves. For its part, China is nervous that the value of the US dollar may be sliding downwards.

Since the early 1970s, when US president Richard Nixon began to open diplomatic discussions with China, relations between the two countries have strengthened. In recent years, China has continued to trade amicably with the US and has shown support for America's stand against terrorism.

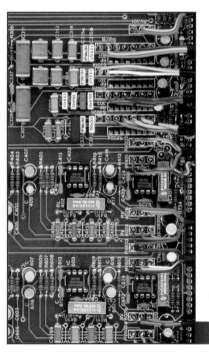

China has invested in the US by setting up numerous companies. Many US computer companies have also invested heavily in China, regarding the Chinese to have excellent technical talents.

Despite being closely linked financially to China, the US does not want to become too close to China diplomatically. China is after all, a one-party communist state, with a poor record in human rights. But in general, both China and the US are looking for co-operation, not confrontation. China, for example, has been keen to show its support for the US in its stance against terrorism and nuclear-proliferation. Both see stability as a key to prosperity. Another important factor in their relationship is their trading agreements with Japan – creating a powerful triangular arrangement, given that the US and Japan are the largest two economies in the world, and China is the sixth largest, and rising.

OTHER PLAYERS

China has always had a tricky relationship with its northern neighbour, Russia, especially since the Sino-Soviet split in 1960. Both are major countries, with the potential to be superpowers. Currently, relationships between China and Russia are cordial: they signed a friendship and co-operation treaty in 2001. China has already found Russia to be a good source for weapons and military technology, and in the future Russia could play an increasingly important role as a supplier of oil. Significantly, after Hu Jintao became president of China in March 2003, his first foreign tour took him to Russia, and the Russian president Vladimir Putin returned the visit in October 2004.

The European Union (EU) represents a major market for Chinese goods, and China offers European companies a source of low-cost manufacturing. In 2003, China became the EU's second largest trading partner.

In the future, Russia may deepen its relations with China through the export of oil – a vital resource for China's development.

Can Japan and China bury the hatchet?

Japan's military intervention in China during the 20th century still arouses deep resentment among the Chinese. But since the political and economic thaw that began in 1978, Japan has been investing heavily in China, and has granted it many trading concessions (notably access to technology). It has also donated more aid to China than any other country (for instance to help improve roads and railways). In return, China provides a valuable market for Japan, taking 48 per cent of its exports. China and Japan have many mutual interests, and complement each other neatly: Japan has advanced technology and 'know-how'; while China has excellent and cheap manufacturing facilities to produce the goods. There has been some suggestion that the two countries may find common cause to create a closer partnership, as the global balance of power shifts. For Japan, China offers a valuable East Asian counterweight to American economic and military power. The exchange of tourist traffic between the two countries already shows some indication of this closer relationship, as does the fact that 60,000 Chinese students now study in Japan. Significantly, Japan did not impose sanctions on China after the Tienanmen Square episode. But there are still several issues to be resolved, including disputes of the ownership of a number of islands (such as the Senkaku or Diaoyutai islands) – and memories of the past.

A delegation from the People's Republic of China is formally seated at the United Nations in 1971 (left).
UN Secretary-General Kofi Annan meets with Wang Guangya, the PRC's permanent representative to the United Nations (below).

THE WORLD STAGE

China joined the United Nations (UN) in 1971, and is one of the five permanent members of its Security Council. It also took Taiwan's seat at the International Monetary Fund and World Bank in 1980. After 15 years of negotiations – and with the support of the USA, the EU and particularly Japan – China joined the World Trade Organisation in 2001, alongside Taiwan.

China is not a member of the Group of Eight (G-8), representing the world's top industrial nations, whose leaders meet regularly for high-level discussions. However, China has been invited to attend as an observer and is likely to receive an offer of membership before long. This is logical, as China now has a bigger economy than at least two of the G-8 members, Italy and Canada.

Meanwhile, China is a member of the Group of 20 (G-20), which contains the G-8 countries, plus 12 of the world's most industrialised countries, and its main developing countries. Among them are two other major emerging economies, India and Brazil, with which China is developing ever closer relations. Together, India, Brazil and China now present a formidable block in trade negotiations. This was seen, for example, at the World Trade Organisation's meeting of ministers at Cancun, Mexico, in 2003, when members of the G-20, led by India, Brazil and China, made a strong case for a better deal for developing countries. In some ways, this is the environment in which China – a communist country, still struggling to shake off Third-World status – seems most at ease.

THE NEW SUPERPOWER?

Since the collapse of the Soviet Union, there has been just one superpower in the world: the USA. The US has the world's largest economy and the world's most sophisticated and powerful military force. It also has a lifestyle and culture that many people envy and admire. History shows, however, that no empire or superpower lasts forever. Over time, others might grow to rival and perhaps to challenge it. China has many of the attributes that could make it into a global superpower. It has the size, the population, the wealth and the drive. Much of its strength has developed very quickly. Is this strength set to continue? Is China destined to take a leading role in the world?

If China can maintain its development, it is set to play a leading role in the global economy for many years.

INDUSTRIAL BASE

China has now become the industrial powerhouse of East Asia – by offering low-cost manufacturing to the world, on a scale that has never previously been matched. In addition, China has the advantage of history: it can profit from the markets – both within the region and globally – already developed by its Asian neighbours.

China already seems to be moving into phase two of industrial development. It has proved that it can manufacture goods cheaply and well; now it is developing its own talents in technology. And by some predictions, China may become the world's largest economy, overtaking the USA, as early as 2020.

What constitutes a superpower?
- Economic strength, and global reach in trade (China certainly has this, but its current prosperity may be vulnerable).
- Military power and an ability to exert this globally (China does not have this yet, but is using its powerful economic position to modernise and upgrade its forces).
- Superpower size: geographical and population (China certainly has these).
- Global cultural influence (China's influence may not yet be profound, but it is widespread).
- A dynamic desire to be a global force and world leader (China does not appear to have this… yet).

MILITARY STRENGTH

China has nuclear weapons. It also has the world's largest army, with a total of 2.3 million regular troops – nearly twice as many as the USA. But in general, its weapons – like machine guns, tanks, missiles, ships and jet fighters – are estimated to be technologically 20 years behind those of the US.

This is set to change: as China becomes wealthier it is investing in more sophisticated weapons, ships and aircraft, largely with Russian assistance. But, like every other country, it has to balance the cost of improving its military strength against other priorities, such as education and healthcare for its people. It also has to assess what it might need weapons for. At present, its prime military concern is the defence of its borders, and controlling civil disobedience. It also has to be able to stand up against the possibility of some future attack by another nuclear power. It is impossible to tell where military investment might go in the future but, with the possible exception of reclaiming Taiwan, no foreign adventures are likely at present.

China has the world's largest army – despite having very few conflicts at present to contend with.

The Chinese space programme

China became the third nation to put a man in space in 2003, when astronaut Yang Yiwei rode the Shenzhou 5 ('Divine Vessel' 5), mounted on a 'Long March' rocket. The first Chinese satellite was put in orbit in 1970, broadcasting the Maoist song 'The East is Red' to the Universe. China has since become a leader in satellite technology and launch systems – putting up its own satellites (including military ones) as well as foreign, commercial ones. Future plans include further manned flights, a large space telescope, exploration of the moon, a space station served by a space shuttle, and even space tourism.

Like the US and the USSR during the 'Space Race' of the 1960s, China sets great store by its space programme: although the costs are huge, the space programme will demonstrate to the world China's growing technological prowess, and what the Chinese, under a communist government, are capable of achieving. China has a firm belief that, although the USA and USSR accomplished many of these objectives decades ago, with experience and investment, it can soon become a leader in space technology.

AMBITION

China does not see itself as a global policeman. It may have sent troops abroad as part of a United Nations force, to Haiti for instance, but this was for a peace-keeping mission. China, generally, refrains from meddling in other nations' affairs, and expects other nations to treat it the same way. In 2004, the Chinese government suggested that it would promote its foreign policy with the slogan '*heping jueqi*' ('peaceful rise'). China officially declares its respect for the sovereignty of other nations, preferring to concentrate on its own political stability and wellbeing. There have been exceptions to this rule in the past: in the 1960s and 1970s China attempted to meddle in the affairs of regional neighbours, such as Vietnam, Cambodia, Laos and Indonesia, and in communist movements in Africa. In the 1960s, it forged a close tie with Albania. But these ventures generally proved unsatisfactory and were shortlived.

Preventing atrocities

This leads to the question: does China want to be a superpower? Certainly, at present, China seems to have too many problems of its own to want to start throwing its weight around abroad. In China itself, the question of being a superpower is generally greeted with some disbelief. The Chinese raise questions about the question itself. Is it being suggested that China might be a future superpower because the US would like to portray it as such – as a potential threat to US power? If the world believes that China does pose a threat to the current superpower balance (so the Chinese argument goes), this might help to justify the USA's own aggressive policies in defence of its superpower status.

China's history suggests that it would not want to be a global power. Apart from establishing security from its immediate neighbours, China is not an aggressive nation.

The rise of the Chinese economy: who wins, who loses?

China is now the world's largest producer of garlic. From 1997 to 2002, China increased its garlic exports to the US from US $42,000 to US $20.5 million. When grocers in the USA found that they could import far cheaper garlic from China, the value of California's garlic crop fell by US $70 million. This is a familiar story. All around the world – and especially in the USA – local industries have been decimated by the arrival of cheap Chinese goods.

Yet, many American companies – such as Nike, Timberland, Kodak, Motorola and General Motors – have taken advantage of the low Chinese labour costs to shift their manufacturing to China. This causes US workers to suffer as their factories close and they lose their jobs; but Chinese factory workers win because they get more jobs. Ultimately, if the US imports more Chinese goods than it exports to China, it ends up with a debt, or 'balance of payments deficit'. Recently this deficit was running at about US $124 billion a year.

That said, the traffic is not always one-way. For example, Brazil has profited from China's need for iron ore, steel, leather and soya beans. Advanced countries can also sell technological and training skills to China.

41

Are Russian president Vladimir Putin (left) and Indian prime minister Manmohan Singh (right) looking to exert superpower status?

OTHER CONTENDERS

If China does not wish to step up to superpower status, are there other countries or regions that might? The European Union (EU) has many of the necessary attributes in terms of size and economic strength. Several of its members – notably Britain, France, the Netherlands and Spain – have been aggressive empire-builders in the past, and still retain a belief in their global influence. But the founding inspiration of the EU was to promote peace rather than the projection of power.

Russia was a superpower until the collapse of communism in 1990. It retains some hope of recovering this position, but Russia probably no longer has the economic or military strength to achieve this. India, the second-most populous nation on Earth, has undergone a rapid rise in prosperity in recent years, in a manner that has parallels with China. With the advantages of low labour costs and a talent for hi-tech industries, it saw an 8 per cent growth rate in 2003-4. But India has never shown any ambition to achieve superpower status.

Can China have global influence on world culture?

One aspect of America's superpower status is its cultural influence on the world. This is not just in fizzy-drinks and fast-food outlets; it is also in films, television programmes, popular music and fashion. Can China ever match that? Chinese culture has been spreading around the globe since ancient times, with its trade in silk, and, later, porcelain and tea. Chinese emigration helped to spread a taste for Chinese food, and latterly there has been a growing worldwide interest in Chinese martial arts, such as tai chi, in the art of spatial organisation called 'feng shui', and in Chinese herbal medicine and acupuncture. China knows the value of this culture as a tool of understanding, and a source of commercial products. China is also prepared to meet the world half-way, by mounting events such as the Shanghai Grand Prix and the Olympic Games. As China's economic power grows, so too will its engagement in world culture.

42

A DIFFERENT ANALYSIS

Perhaps, therefore, there are no new candidates for future superpower status. Perhaps the very concept of superpowers is outdated. Political analysts argue that it might be more realistic to see the world in terms of competing regions. It has been suggested that, in the future, the world will be divided into three regional power centres – an analysis called 'tri-regionalism'. One of these would be the US, in association with all the countries in the Americas; another would be the EU, perhaps in conjunction with Russia; and another would be East Asia, clustering around China, and perhaps in association with India. If superpower status is a thing of the past, perhaps these three regions will come to influence the world of future generations. Whatever the argument, China is likely to remain a force to be reckoned with, and a major player on the world stage.

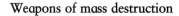

Weapons of mass destruction

China tested its first atomic bomb in 1964 and an H-bomb in 1967. It has since developed and upgraded its nuclear arsenal, and is now estimated to have at least 450 nuclear warheads. China also has missiles with a range of 11,000 km, thus capable of reaching just about any strategic target in the world. However, China, along with the four other original nuclear powers – the USA, Russia, France and Britain – signed the Nuclear Non-Proliferation Treaty in 1968. For its part, China is committed to reducing its nuclear stockpiles and preventing the spread of nuclear weapons – although China did help Pakistan to develop nuclear weapons in the 1990s. China denies that it has any chemical and biological weapons, but this is disputed.

China has come a long way since the days of imperial rule. Future generations will enjoy a better standard of living and a freer society than their ancestors.

CHRONOLOGY

1368 – The Ming dynasty began (1368-1644). In 1514, the first European traders arrived in China, from Portugal; by 1557, they had established a trading station at Macau.

1644 – The Qing dynasty, China's last imperial dynasty (1644-1912) was founded by the Manchus of northern China (Manchuria).

1839 – The First Opium War (1839-42) broke out after Chinese officials seized large quantities of illegal opium from British traders in Guangzhou. China lost both this and the Second Opium War (1856-60). Under the Treaty of Nanking (1842) and the Treaty of Tianjin (1858), China had to give up some of its territorial sovereignty to Western countries. This episode began the 'Century of Humiliation'.

1895 – At the end of the First Sino-Japanese War (1894-95), China had lost Korea, Taiwan and a part of Manchuria to the Japanese.

1900 – The anti-Western Boxer Rebellion was put down by European, American and Japanese troops.

1911 – The last emperor of China, the five-year-old boy Puyi, was overthrown by republican revolutionaries. The following year China was declared a republic, with Dr Sun Yat-sen as its provisional president.

1919 – The 'May Fourth' movement began when 3,000 Chinese students gathered in Tienanmen

Square, Beijing, to protest against the Treaty of Versailles, awarding treaty-port concessions to the Japanese.

1921 – The Chinese Communist Party (CCP) was founded, with Mao Zedong among its first members. Sun Yat-sen's Nationalist Party, the Kuomintang (KMT), formed an alliance with the Communists, but turned against them when Chiang Kai-shek took over the leadership of the KMT following Sun Yat-sen's death in 1925.

1934 – The communist 'Red Army' escaped Kuomintang (KMT) forces in Jiangxi Province and began the 'Long March' (1934-35), a trek of more than 9,000 kilometres to reach safety in Shaanxi province. Mao emerged as the Communists' leader at this time.

1937 – The Second Sino-Japanese War (1937-45) began with the Japanese invasion of China from Manchuria. In the 'Rape of Nanking' (1937-38), some 300,000 Chinese citizens were slaughtered.

1945 – After the Japanese defeat at the end of the Second World War, the Communists and the KMT (Chiang Kai-shek's Nationalists) resumed their civil war for the control of China.

1949 – The Communists won the civil war. On 1 October the People's Republic of China was proclaimed, with Mao Zedong as the head of state. Chiang Kai-shek and the KMT retreated to Taiwan to set up a rival government, supported by the USA.

1950 – China's army came to the aid of North Korea as it faced defeat by United Nations forces during the Korean War (1950-53).

1957 – Mao launched the 'Great Leap Forward', a campaign of rapid changes to agriculture and industry. It ended three years later in disaster and mass starvation due to crop failure.

1959 – A revolt in Chinese-occupied Tibet was crushed by the Chinese, and the Dalai Lama fled to India.

1964 – China tested its first atomic bomb.

1966 – Mao launched the 'Cultural Revolution', aimed at radically transforming Chinese society. It resulted in a period of turmoil, orchestrated by the fanatical Red Guards. Order was restored in 1969 by the People's Liberation Army led by Lin Biao.

1971 – China joined the United Nations.

1972 – Richard Nixon became the first US president to visit Communist China, and held meetings with Mao Zedong and prime minister Zhou Enlai. This represented a significant shift in big-power politics at the height of the Cold War.

1976 – Mao died at the age of 82. The moderate Deng Xiaoping emerged as the most influential politician in government.

1978 – Deng Xiaoping announced a change in government economic policy, opening the door to a limited market economy, private enterprise and foreign investment. This marked the start of China's rapid economic development.

1979 – The first Special Economic Zones (SEZs) were set up to encourage foreign investment. The government also introduced a 'one child' policy to curb population growth.

1989 – Economic and political reforms came to a halt when the government crushed a huge pro-democracy demonstration in Tienanmen Square on 4 June.

1993 – Deng Xiaoping announced the resumption of economic reforms. Jiang Zemin became president.

1997 – China regained Hong Kong from the British.

1999 – The Chinese government broke up a gathering of Falun Gong followers in Beijing and then banned the religious sect altogether.

2001 – President Jiang Zemin announced his 'Three Represents' policy, under which the Chinese Communist Party would open up membership to business people for the first time. China joined the World Trade Organisation.

2002 – An attempt by the Chinese government to cover up an outbreak of the Severe Acute Respiratory Syndrome (SARS) allowed the killer disease to spread. SARS caused huge damage to China's economy and tourist industry until it was finally contained in 2004.

2003 – Jiang Zemin stepped down as president and was replaced by Hu Jintao, with Wen Jiabao as premier (prime minister). China launched its first manned space mission.

2004 – China hosted a number of high-profile international events, including the first Shanghai Grand Prix. The Maglev, Shanghai's magnetic-levitation train, was inaugurated.

2008 – Beijing will host the Olympic Games.

ORGANISATIONS AND GLOSSARY

Association of South East Asian Nations (ASEAN) – This alliance was founded in 1967 to promote economic growth, peace and stability in the region. It now has ten members: Indonesia, Malaysia, the Philippines, Thailand, Singapore, Brunei, Vietnam, Laos, Myanmar (Burma) and Cambodia.

Authoritarian – Strict, demanding obedience, and usually refusing to listen to argument or criticism.

Capitalist – A society or an individual that uses capital (money or property) to make a profit. A capitalist system involves private ownership (of, for instance, property) as opposed to state-ownership. The term 'capitalism' is often used as the opposite of communism.

Collective farm – Under communist regimes, agricultural land was taken over by the State and reorganised into huge collective farms, to improve efficiency.

Communism – An idealistic system of government devised principally by the German theorist Karl Marx (1818-83). The intention was to remove the inequalities of society, so that everyone could have an equal share in wealth and opportunities. A communist government would take over all land, property, workplaces and sources of money, and ensure that these were redistributed equally.

Consumer society – A term that emerged in the 1960s to describe people in well-off capitalist countries whose lives revolve around shopping and owning possessions.

Dissent – Disagreeing with the majority viewpoint.

Dissident – A persistent critic; someone who dissents. The term is used in particular of people in communist or authoritarian countries who criticise the government, and put themselves at great risk by doing so.

Domestic market – All the buyers and traders in one's own country (also called the 'home market'), as opposed to the buyers and traders abroad (the export market).

Dynasty – A family of rulers or leaders that passes power down from one generation to the next.

European Union (EU) – This grouping of European countries began in 1951 when six countries agreed to promote peace and prosperity by removing barriers to trade and forming a 'common market'. It evolved through several stages – e.g., European Economic Community (EEC), European Community (EC) – before becoming the European Union in 1991. It now has 25 members.

Free market – Where trade is regulated entirely by supply and demand, and without interference from government, it is said to be a 'free market'.

Government bonds – Bonds are certificates that people can buy as an investment. The bonds usually earn interest, increasing in value over time. Governments issue bonds – called government bonds, or treasury bonds – as a way of borrowing money.

Group of Eight (G-8) – Eight of the world's leading industrial nations meet regularly for high-level discussions. Currently the G-8's members are Canada, France, Germany, Italy, Japan, Russia, the UK and the USA; the EU is also treated as a member. China has been invited to attend as an observer, and may well be invited to join the group.

Human rights – This broad term is used to refer to the essential rights or freedoms that many people believe any individual should have in a free society. They include the freedom of speech, the freedom of movement, and the freedom of association, as well as the right to fair and impartial justice.

Imperial – The adjective used in relation to an empire or emperor.

Infrastructure – All the systems used to move people, goods and information around a country, and to supply power (e.g. electricity). Roads, railways, airports, telephone systems and power stations are all part of the infrastructure.

International Monetary Fund (IMF) – An agency of the United Nations, the IMF was established to promote international trade and development.

North Atlantic Treaty Organisation (NATO) – NATO was founded in 1949 as a defence organisation that brought together the USA, Canada and their allies in Western Europe to face the military threat posed by the Soviet Union. It now has 26 member countries.

Political prisoner – A prisoner who is arrested and held for expressing his or her political beliefs. Political prisoners are usually found in countries with authoritarian regimes that do not tolerate opposition.

Protectionism – If a government wishes to protect its own industries from foreign competition, it can introduce a variety of measures (such as customs duties, quotas and other trade barriers) to put foreign produce at a disadvantage. This is called 'protectionism'.

Republic – A country that is ruled by the people. The term is often used in a country where the monarchy has been removed: instead of a king/queen, or emperor/empress, the head of state of a republic is usually a president.

Sanctions – When the government of a country is thought to have misbehaved in some major way, other countries may show their displeasure by imposing trade sanctions. This means that they refuse to trade with that country, in the hope that the sanctions will pressure the government into changing its policies.

Sino- – A prefix meaning Chinese, usually used in conjunction with another nationality (Sino-Russian, Sino-Japanese). The term has come through French, Latin and Arabic, but probably has the same root as the word 'China'.

Slump – A large, long and painful downturn in the economy of a country, a region or the world.

Special Economic Zones (SEZs) – Industrial zones especially established in and around certain Chinese cities after 1979 to provide favourable conditions for manufacturing export products, and for foreign companies investing in China.

Totalitarian – An adjective used to describe a government that is extremely strict and authoritarian, and wants to have total control of everything.

Treaty ports – The set of ports in China (and elsewhere in East Asia) where foreign merchants could operate under their own laws and taxation systems. Many of these were established by the 'unequal treaties', such as the Treaty of Nanking (1842) and the Treaties of Tianjin (1858), which caused deep resentment in China.

United Nations (UN) – An international organisation founded in 1945 to promote peace, security and economic development, the UN is composed of most of the countries of the world. At the heart of the UN is the Security Council, which has five permanent members (China, France, Russia, the United Kingdom and the United States); a further ten posts in the Security Council are taken by other countries elected for two years by the General Assembly.

World Trade Organisation (WTO) – The WTO was established in 1995. Based in Geneva, with 145 countries as members, its task is to monitor national trading policies, to help to settle trading disputes and to try to reduce tariffs and other barriers to trade.

INDEX

48

Photo Credits:
Abbreviations: l-left, r-right, b-bottom, t-top, c-centre, m-middle. Front cover main, ml, c and back cover t, 7tl, 7bl, 7br, 11mr, 15tr, 19br, 25bl, 33br – Flat Earth. Front cover mr, 8bl, 21 tr, 28mr, 28bl, 35mr – George Michael. 1ml, 8ml, 14tr, 15ml, 20br, 27mr, 38tl, 41tr, 44tr – Corel. 1c, 40bl – Christopher Lowden. 1mr, 9tr, 9trm, 9trb, 21m, 21b, 23bl, 45bl – Jian Shuo Wang. 2-3b, 3tr, 10br, 11bl, 17br, 23tr, 25tl – Select Pictures. 2bl, 2ml, 4tr, 22bl, 43br – Affordable Stock Photography. 4bl, 5br, 8tr, 29tr, 39mr, 42br – ©Dennis Cox/ChinaStock. 7m, 13mr – PBD. 12bl, 14bm, 44bl – www.informationwar.org. 12br, 13bl – ©ChinaStock. 16bl – ©Wu Yinxian/ChinaStock. 17tl – ©Lu Houmin/ChinaStock. 18bl – AP/Wide World Photos. 19tl, 19ml – US National Archive and Records Administration. 24tr, 33mr – Photodisc. 24 mr, 24br, 45 tr – Arup. 26tl – ©Liu Liqun/ChinaStock. 30br – Gilles Sabrie / WorldPictureNews. 31br – Courtesy of the Falun Dafa Information Center. 32tc – Myles Chilton / WorldPictureNews. 34ml – Josh Stephenson / WorldPictureNews. 36tr – Paul Morse/www.whitehouse.gov. 36mr – Eric Draper/www.whitehouse.gov. 36bl – Ingram Publishing. 37tr – epa photo / AFI / Normunds Mezins. 38mr – UN Photo / WorldPictureNews. 40mr – Corbis. 42tl – Amit Kumar / WorldPictureNews.